WHY DID ARSENE WENGER CROSS THE ROAD?

WHY DID ARSENE WENGER CROSS THE ROAD?

It's by far the greatest
FOOTBALL JOKEBOOK
the world has ever seen ...

J A C K   B R E M N E R

BANTAM PRESS

LONDON · TORONTO · SYDNEY · AUCKLAND · JOHANNESBURG

TRANSWORLD PUBLISHERS
61–63 Uxbridge Road, London W5 5SA
a division of The Random House Group Ltd

RANDOM HOUSE AUSTRALIA (PTY) LTD
20 Alfred Street, Milsons Point, Sydney,
New South Wales 2061, Australia

RANDOM HOUSE NEW ZEALAND LTD
18 Poland Road, Glenfield, Auckland 10, New Zealand

RANDOM HOUSE SOUTH AFRICA (PTY) LTD
Isle of Houghton, Corner of Boundary Road and Carse O'Gowrie,
Houghton 2198, South Africa

Published 2005 by Bantam Press, a division of Transworld Publishers

A catalogue record for this book is available from the British Library.
ISBN 0593 055322

Designed by www.carrstudio.co.uk
Printed in Great Britain by Bath Press
1 3 5 7 9 10 8 6 4 2

Papers used by Transworld Publishers are natural, recyclable products made from
wood grown in sustainable forests. The manufacturing processes conform to the
environmental regulations of the country of origin.

Contents

Introduction

I sincerely hope that you have not bought *Why Did Arsène Wenger Cross the Road?* as a Christmas present for your Aunt Agatha. Unless, that is, your Aunt Agatha enjoys a damned good rib-tickler involving Posh Spice, bike sheds, Kit-Kats and a semi-naked Sven-Goran Eriksson with his Spiderman-themed briefs round his ankles. If she's anything like my Aunt Agatha, I'd pop the book straight into a safe box and hide it under the bed next to your secret Abi Titmuss scrapbook – and then sit tight and wait until she is safely back on the train to Littlehampton. Get her a tightly fitting whalebone corset instead. She'll take more pleasure from that. It'll remind her of a golden age in our history when Britons declined to wear baseball caps and tracksuits, and women were yet to address each other as 'mate'. Aunt Agatha would only have to read to the end of page 1 of this collection to find the hairs on her chin standing on end in moral indignation at the state of the nation. 'How can they publish such muck and smut?' I can hear her bristling. 'Who reads this dung?'

When I sat down to write this introduction I was very briefly tempted to try to persuade you that the book you are holding in your hand is some kind of mini-classic of modern English literature, one of just a handful on the shelves of our bookshops with the capacity to deflect the course of our lives a little, forcing us to reassess our values and look at the world around us in a different way. Fair enough, the book can be a little crude and bawdy in places; but this, I felt, was a modest price to pay in assembling a collection that seeks to celebrate the distinctively British wit and humour of the everyday man on the Clapham omnibus en route to and from the Association Football ground. Besides, I reassured myself, even the great fourteenth-century poet Geoffrey Chaucer found it difficult to resist a good farty joke . . . But then I flicked through the text, and the very first entry my eyes alighted upon read as follows: *Q: How can you tell when a Sunderland lass is having an orgasm? A: She drops her chips.*

Now, you could mount a plausible argument to claim that this little gag could just as well have been lifted straight out of *The Miller's Tale* or *The Wife of Bath's Tale* and tarted up for modern readers. But, quite honestly, who am I trying to kid? Let's call a shovel a shovel: *Why Did Arsène Wenger Cross the Road?* is nothing more than a compilation of rude, gross, silly, mocking, infantile and downright

nasty little jokes that the more mature amongst us ceased to find funny when they were about sixteen years old.

The allure of a fart or bottom joke, however, is a powerful one, and should not be underestimated. I once witnessed a former Archbishop of Canterbury biting his lower lip, desperately fighting back a snot explosion as he buried his head in his vestments after one of his flock had cut the cheese during a Good Friday sermon at Westminster Abbey. It is one of my fondest memories, and the moral of the lesson was clear, namely, that none of us, not even faith leaders, are above tittering at an inopportune trouser raspberry or a good willy gag.

Like its sister publication *Shit Ground No Fans* (a compilation of rude, gross, silly, mocking, infantile and downright nasty little football chants), *Why Did Arsène Wenger Cross the Road?* owes a tremendous debt of gratitude to thousands of puerile football fans up and down our great country. Without their magnificent and frankly childish commitment to mocking as many of their fellow citizens as possible – not to mention some of our hairy and smelly cousins on the Continent – this book would be nothing more than a wad of blank pages in an elegantly designed jacket; a Ferrari with no engine, if you will.

Why Did Arsène Wenger Cross the Road? is the logical follow-up to *Shit Ground*.

When Britain's several million football fans have finished hurling comic banter and vile abuse at each other on a Saturday afternoon, they file out of the nation's stadiums and head straight into the nearest pub or on to the local transport network to continue the ribaldry in another form – cracking jokes about their rivals and neighbours. This book seeks to record those jokes for future generations (so that they might laugh *at* us, not *with* us).

Like *Shit Ground*, this book, I'm afraid, also makes no concessions to political correctness, weak hearts, social niceties, sensitive feelings, class divisions, delicate constitutions, national, regional or civic pride, and neither does it tremble before the wrath of wronged gods or the good people of Wearside . . . or Merseyside . . . or east London . . . or Glasgow . . . or Swansea . . . On the contrary, it takes great pride and satisfaction in upsetting as many people as possible in the ancient and noble pursuit of a damned good belly laugh at someone else's expense. If you are easily offended, I suggest you put this book down now; but if you have a humourless, hairy-chinned aunt you'd like to upset, then get wrapping.

Acknowledgements

There are a handful of people I'd like to thank for their help in putting together this book. The publishing team at Transworld, from designers through to sales people, have been excellent; and I'd like to offer special thanks to editor Doug Young, who is a pleasure to work (and lunch) with. My agent Araminta Whitley at LAW, meanwhile, should be made a member of the Most Noble Order of the Garter – for services to me – without further delay. It's an incredible oversight by the Queen to have ignored her claims for so long and, using the strongest language decency permits, I shall be writing to Her Majesty to tell her as much. Scientists couldn't build a better agent than Araminta. I'd also like to thank her extremely efficient and cheerful assistant Lizzie Jones.

Team by Team

Aberdeen

Q: How do you know an Aberdeen fan has burgled your house?
A: The bin is empty and the dog is pregnant.

Magistrate to Aberdeen fan before heading into court: 'Are you the defence lawyer?'
Aberdeen fan: 'No, I'm the bloke who smashed up the police car.'

A man in a Scottish pub shouts out that he has a great joke about Aberdeen.

One of his fellow drinkers interrupts: 'I should warn you that I'm six foot four, a seventeen-stone body-builder, my friend Buster McTyson here is a black belt in karate and my other friend Dave McShite has just been released from Barlinnie jail after ten years for GBH. We are all Aberdeen fans. Are you sure you want to tell this joke?'

The man replies: 'No, not if I have to explain it three times.'

Arsenal

Little Tommy: 'Mum, I want to be an Arsenal season-ticket holder when I grow up.'
Mum: 'Well, you'll have to make your mind up, Tommy – you can't do both.'

Q: Why do Arsenal fans whistle when they are sitting on the toilet?
A: So they know which end to wipe.

A man walks into a bar, drunk as a skunk, and shouts: 'All Arsenal fans are arseholes!'
    A man sitting in the corner protests: 'Oi! I take offence at that!'
    'Why? Are you an Arsenal fan?' asks the drunk.
    'No, I'm an arsehole.'

Q: Why do NASA send their astronauts to train at Highbury?
A: It's the only place in the world with no atmosphere.

Q: Why is an Arsenal fan like a three-pin plug?
A: They're both completely useless in Europe.

Patrick Vieira walks into a pub, and the landlord says: 'A pint of your usual, Pat?'
Vieira replies: 'No, just a half, then I'm off.'

Aston Villa

Q: What happens when an Aston Villa fan takes a Viagra pill?
A: He gets a bit taller.


```
--- News report
---------------
```
Villa Park was broken into last night, and the entire contents of the trophy room were stolen. West Midlands police are looking for a man with a claret-and-blue carpet.

Q: What do you call the useless piece of skin on the end of an Aston Villa player's dick?
A: An Aston Villa player.

Birmingham City

Q: Why did God make Birmingham City supporters stink?
A: So blind people could laugh at them, too.

Life as a Birmingham City fan? You lose some, you draw some.
(Apologies to Jasper Carrott.)

A Birmingham City fan walks into a clothes shop in the Bullring to buy some new gear for a night out on the town.

'Kipper tie?' asks the assistant in his Brummie accent.

'Oh, that's very kind of you,' says the fan. 'I'll have milk and two sugars, ta.'

Blackburn Rovers

Blackburn fan: 'Hey, babe, I'd love to get into your pants.'
Good-looking intelligent woman: 'Sorry, love, there's one arsehole already in there.'

Q: What's the difference between a Blackburn girl and a Vietnamese pot-bellied pig?
A: About eight pints.

You know you are a Blackburn fan when ...
1. You let your twelve-year-old daughter smoke at the dinner table in front of her kids.

2. You go to your family reunion looking for a date.

3. Your school dance has a crèche.

4. One of your kids was born on a pool table.

5. Your dad walks you to school because you are both in the same year.

6. Your toilet paper has page numbers on it.

Bolton Wanderers

Q: What time do Bolton kick off?
A: About every ten minutes.

Q: Why do Bolton fans have big nostrils?
A: Because they have big fingers.

Are you worried about your financial future?

Face the facts, you're not getting any younger, and we all have to think about our standard of living once our careers are over. Are you well past your best but looking for a bit of cash on Easy Street?

You are? Well, read on, because you are eligible for the **Bolton Life Plan**! After sailing through an irrelevant medical, Bolton will pay you in excess of £30,000 a week, give you a free house, a luxury sports car and as much time on England's finest golf courses as you could wish. You don't even have to play football if you don't want to.

But don't take only our word for it. Read the following endorsements by some of our newly signed-up clients:

'When I'm retired, I now know that my family will be financially secure. It's a real load off the mind.' *Ivan*, Bolton.

'I have no hesitation in recommending the Bolton Life Plan to all over-the-hill players.' *Gary*, Bolton.

'I couldn't believe the money these twats were prepared to offer me. They still pay me even though I can barely walk.' *Fernando*, Bolton.

'Silly arseholes, I'm absolutely loaded now.' *Youri*, Seychelles.

'F**k off or I'll gob in your face.' *El-Hadji*, Bolton airport.

Cardiff

Two young Cardiff fans come home with a football, and their mother asks where they got it.

'We found it,' say the young tearaways.

'Now, lads, are you absolutely sure it was lost?' asks Mum suspiciously.

'Yea, deffo. We saw the people looking for it.'

Q: How long does it take a Cardiff lass to have a shit?
A: About nine months.

A Cardiff fan gets on to the bus holding her four-week-old baby. The bus driver recoils in horror, saying: 'Blimey, that's one f**king ugly baby!' The woman pays her fare and starts to sob as she takes a seat at the back of the bus.

The man next to her asks her gently: 'Are you all right, love? Whatever's up?'

'The bus driver has just been really rude to me,' she moans.

'I can see you are a Cardiff fan and all, but there's no excuse for public servants like him to go about insulting people in that way. Why don't you go and give him a piece of your mind, and I'll hold your monkey for you.'

First Cardiff fan: 'Are you shearing that sheep?'
Second Cardiff fan: 'No, bugger off and get your own.'

A Reading fan, an Oxford fan and a Cardiff fan are walking through the countryside when they see a sheep stuck in a gate.

The Reading fan says: 'God, I wish that was Jordan.'

The Oxford fan says: 'I wish it was Kylie Minogue.'

The Cardiff fan says: 'I just wish it was dark.'

Celtic

A Celtic fan is walking home from a match in his club colours when he ducks into a pub for a quick pint, only to discover that it is a fiercely Rangers establishment.

A deadly silence descends before the barman leans over the counter and says: 'In this pub, we like to play the "Celtic Dice Game". If you roll a one we punch you once, if you roll a two we punch you twice, and so on up to five.'

'What happens if I roll a six?' asks the hapless Celtic follower.

'You get to roll again, my friend.'

Q: How many Celtic supporters does it take to stop a moving bus?

A: Never enough.

Q: How do you get a one-armed Celtic fan down from a tree?

A: Wave to him.

Q: What does Celtic really stand for?

A: Celtic Even Lost To Inverness Caledonian.

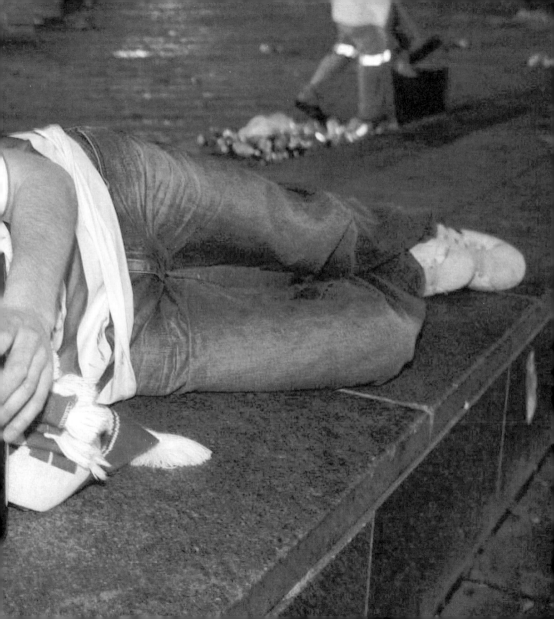

Charlton

Q: How many Charlton fans does it take to change a lightbulb?
A: Both of them.

Q: What do you call a dead Charlton fan in a closet?
A: Last year's winner of the hide-and-seek contest.

Q: What do you say to a Charlton fan at the peak of his career?
A: Big Mac and fries, please.

A doctor told a football fan with a heart condition to try to avoid unnecessary excitement, so he started supporting Charlton.

Chelsea

Q: Two Chelsea fans jump off a cliff. Which one hits the ground first?
A: Who gives a f**k?

A mega-rich Russian oil baron had a son and heir whom he loved very much, and on the young lad's sixth birthday he said to him: 'Boy, I am very proud of you. Whatever you want for your birthday, you shall have.'

'Daddy, I would like an airplane,' the boy said. So his father bought him British Airways.

On the morning of his seventh birthday, the unshaven tycoon took the boy to one side again and said: 'Son, you continue to be a great source of pride and joy. What would you like this year?'

'A boat would be super, Dad.' So his father bought him *QE2*.

On his eighth birthday, the baron asked his lad: 'Son, you are turning out to be a wonderful child and a worthy heir to my fortune. What can I get for you this year?'

'Well, I have always loved cartoons, as you know, Pops.' So his father bought him Disney Studios and the rights to all their films.

The following year, the baron repeated his affection and admiration for the young boy. 'Son, you are an inspiration to us all. Once again, name your present and I will buy it for you.'

'Dad, cartoons are everything to me. I'd love a Mickey Mouse outfit.' So his father bought him Chelsea Football Club.

Two men are walking through a cemetery when they come upon a tombstone that reads:

'Here lies Colin Askew, a good man and a Chelsea fan.'

One says to the other: 'Crikey, when the hell did they start putting two people in one grave?'

Q: What is the difference between the Elephant Man and Chelsea striker Mateja Kezman?

A: The Elephant Man has a better chance of scoring.

Arsène Wenger, Sir Alex Ferguson, and Jose Mourinho are killed in a plane crash on the way to a UEFA summit meeting in Switzerland. As they enter the Pearly Gates, the Almighty greets them, turning to Wenger first of all and asking: 'Tell me, Arsène, what qualities do you most cherish in people?'

'Humility, respect and love,' replies the Frenchman.

'I like what I hear. Come and sit at my left hand,' says God, who then puts the same question to Sir Alex.

'Courage, fortitude and generosity,' replies the Taggart lookalike.

'You talk a great deal of sense, Scotsman. Come and sit at my right hand.'

God then turns to Mourinho, who is staring at him contemptuously. God asks him: 'Whatever is the problem, my little Portuguese friend?'

'You're sitting in my seat, you big twat.'

Crystal Palace

It is a beautiful spring afternoon when a Crystal Palace fan walks into a pub with his dog just as the football results are being read out on the television. The announcer says that Palace have lost 3–0, and the dog immediately rolls over on its back, sticks its legs in the air, makes a strange whimpering noise and plays dead.

'That's amazing,' says the barman. 'What does he do when they win?'

'No idea, I've only had him for eight months,' replies the Palace fan.

Q: How can you tell when Palace are losing?
A: It's five past three.

One day Quasimodo turns to Esmerelda and asks sadly: 'Am I truly the ugliest man alive?'

Esmerelda says: 'Well, Quasi, there's only one way to find out. Go upstairs and ask the magic mirror who is the ugliest man alive, and the mirror will reveal the truth.'

Five minutes later, Quasimodo comes back with a quizzical look on his face and says to Esmerelda: 'Who the f**k is Iain Dowie?'

Dundee/Dundee United

Two Dundee newlyweds go on their honeymoon to Blackpool, but after just a few days the husband returns by himself.

'What's happened to Charleen, son?' his father asks.

'I'm afraid I had to shoot her, Dad.'

The father is shocked. 'Why in heaven did you ever do that, lad?'

'Well, it's embarrassing. I found out that she was a virgin, Dad.'

'Well, that's different,' the father says. 'You did the right thing, my lad. If she isnae good enough for her own folks, she surely isnae good enough for this family.'

Q: How many Dundee fans does it take to change a lightbulb?

A: Trick question – there are no Dundee fans.

Q: What's the definition of a Dundee virgin?

A: A girl who can run faster than her father and brothers.

Everton

An Everton fan goes to the surgery with his wife for a check-up, and the doctor says: 'I am not happy with everything I have seen. I'm afraid I'm going to need a blood sample, a urine sample, a semen sample and a stool sample before you go so that we can carry out some more detailed tests.'

'Blimey, but I feel in the flush of good health, Doctor,' says the shell-shocked Toffees fan. 'Are you sure this is necessary?'

At which point his wife butts in and says: 'Oh, shut up, Wayne, just give the man your underpants and let's get out of here.'

Did you hear the one about the Everton burglar who saw his Wanted poster outside the police station? He went in and applied for the job.

Q: How many Everton fans does it take to eat a hedgehog?

A: Two. One to eat the hedgehog and one to watch for traffic.

Q: What do you call an Everton fan with a job?
A: A pickpocket.

Q: How do you make an Everton fan run faster?
A: Stick a video player under his arm.

Fulham

Q: What's the difference between Craven Cottage and Stonehenge?
A: One is a simple ancient structure which defies attempts to explain its purpose, and the other's a popular attraction in Wiltshire.

Q: Why is it so hot at Fulham games?
A: Because there isn't a fan at Craven Cottage.

Gillingham

Barrister: What gear were you in when the car hit the lamp post?
Gillingham fan: Burberry cap and Reeboks.

Q: What did the Gillingham fan get on his IQ test?
A: Saliva.

Q: How do you kill a Gillingham supporter while he's having a drink?
A: Slam the toilet seat on his head.

Q: What do you call a Gillingham girl without any children?
A: A toddler.

Q: What does a Gillingham girl do with her bum after sex?
A: Sends him out for a Big Mac and a bottle of White Lightning.

Q: What do you call a Gillingham fan in a white shell-suit?
A: The bride.

Glasgow Rangers

Q: What's the difference between a Rangers fan and a bucket of crap?
A: The bucket.

Q: What do you call a Rangers fan in Europe after Christmas?
A: A tourist.

Q. What's blue, red, white and funny?
A: A busload of Rangers supporters going over a cliff.

Q: What does a Rangers fan do after he's just watched his team beat Barcelona?
A: Turns off his Playstation.

Hearts

Q: How can you tell it is a Hearts fan looking through a keyhole?
A: You can see both his eyes.

A young Hearts fan is walking along the 'beach' at Portobello with his mangy, rabid, one-eared, three-legged dog when he finds a magic lamp and rubs it. Out pops a genie, who says: 'You have released me from a thousand years of imprisonment, and for that I shall grant you one wish.'

The Jambo holds his chin for a moment before declaring: 'I love my dog so much that I would like you to restore him to full health and give him back his missing leg and missing ear.'

'Blimey, I'm just a bog-standard genie, not an effing miracle-worker!' exclaims the genie.

'Oh, all right, then, I'd like Hearts to win the SPL just once in my lifetime.'

'Second thoughts, give me another look at that dog.'

Hibernian

Q: What do you call a pregnant Hibs fan?
A: A dope-carrier.

Q: How does a Hibs fan change a lightbulb?
A: He asks the prison guard.

An enormous Hibs fan, six foot six and nineteen stone, is sitting at a bar in Leith one afternoon having a quiet beer when a gay man walks in and sits down next to him. After downing a few beers for courage the gay man turns to the big Hibee and whispers: 'Do you fancy a blow job, big man?' The Hibee is enraged and smacks the poor man off his bar stool, drags him round the back and punches seven shades of shite out of him in the car park before returning to his seat as if nothing had happened.

The barman is stunned and says: 'I've never seen you so angry, Dermot. What in heaven's name did the lad say to you?'

'I'm not sure,' says Big Dermot. 'Something to do with a job.'

Q: What do you call a Hibernian fan in college?
A: The caretaker.

Leeds United

One Leeds fan says to his mate: 'What would you do if you ever won the lottery?'

'That's simple,' he replies. 'I'd buy a controlling interest in Leeds United.'

'Yeah, that's great, but what if you got FOUR numbers right?'

Two men are fishing on a riverbank in a remote area of the countryside on a Saturday afternoon. Out of the blue one turns to the other and says:

'Leeds have lost again.'

The other man is flabbergasted.

'How the heavens do you know that?' he asks.

'Because it's ten to five, stupid.'

Q: Why do people take an instant dislike to Leeds fans?

A: It saves time.

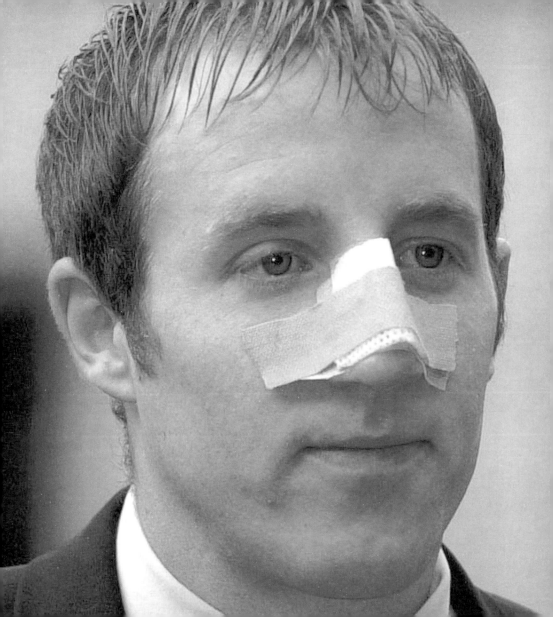

First Leeds fan: Did you hear about Nathan? 'E were found shagging a pig behind t' barn last night.
Second Leeds fan: Female pig, was it?
First Leeds fan: 'Course it were. There's nowt queer about our Nathan.

A Leeds fan goes home for his dinner, and his wife puts a plate of grass on the table in front of him.

'What the effing Nora do you call this?' he asks.

'If it's good enough for thy fancy woman,' replies the wife, 'it's good enough for thee.'

Q: How many Leeds United players does it take to change a lightbulb?
A: Six. One to change the bulb and five to beat the shit out of the old one.

Q: What has seventy thousand arms and an IQ of 170?
A: Elland Road every other Saturday.

Liverpool

Q: Why does the River Mersey run past Liverpool?
A: If it walked, it would get mugged.

Two boys are playing football in a Manchester park when one of them is attacked by a Dobermann pinscher. His friend immediately grabs a plank of wood from a fence, pushes it into the dog's collar and twists it, breaking the beast's neck. A local newspaper reporter taking a stroll through the park sees what has happened, rushes over and takes out his pad and pencil to ask the lads some questions.

As a rough heading he scribbles down: 'Manchester City Fan Saves Friend from Vicious Animal.'

The boy interrupts him, protesting: 'But I'm not a City fan.'

The reporter crosses it out and starts again: 'Manchester United Fan Saves Friend from Vicious Animal.'

The boy interrupts again, saying: 'But I'm not a United fan, either.'

So the reporter asks: 'Well, who the hell do you support, then?'

'Liverpool,' replies the boy.

The reporter starts again: 'Scouse Bastard Kills Family Pet.'

Q: What do you call a Scouse lass who has an abortion?
A: Crime-stopper.

Q: What do you call a Liverpool fan in a three-bedroom semi?

A: A burglar.

A teacher starts a new job at a primary school on Merseyside and, trying to curry some favour on her first day, explains to her class that she is a Liverpool fan. She asks the other Liverpool fans in the room to raise their hand, and everyone does – except for one little girl.

The teacher looks at the girl with surprise and says: 'Tracey, why haven't you put your hand up?'

'Because I'm not a Liverpool fan,' she replies.

A little taken aback, the teacher asks: 'Well, if you're not a Liverpool fan, then who do you support?'

'I'm a Manchester United fan and proud of it,' Tracey says defiantly.

The teacher is astonished. 'Why on earth are you a United fan?' she splutters.

'Because my mum and dad are from Manchester, and they are both United fans, so I'm a United fan, too.'

'For Pete's sake,' says the exasperated teacher. 'That's no reason for you to be a United fan. You don't have to copy everything your parents do all the time. What if your mum was a prostitute and your dad was a drug addict and a car thief, what would you be then?'

'Well,' says Tracey, 'I'd be a Liverpool fan.'

Man in Liverpool shop: 'I'd like to buy a pair of tights for my wife, please.'
Shop assistant: 'Certainly, sir. What size head are you?'

Q: Why should you never run over a Liverpool fan who's on a bike?
A: It's probably *your* bike.

Manchester City

Kevin Keegan took the squad out to a fancy local restaurant in an effort to rebuild team morale after the team had suffered its 457th consecutive defeat at the weekend.

After taking their orders for starters, the waiter says: 'And what would Mr Keegan like for main course?'

'I'll have the lightly grilled halibut in the cream of pepper sauce,' replies Kev.

'Lovely, an excellent choice, Mr Keegan. And what about your vegetables?'

'Oh, don't worry about them; they can have the same as me.'

Q: How many Man City fans does it take to change a lightbulb?
A: None, they're all happy living in the shadows.

Q: What has fourteen arms and an IQ of minus thirty?
A: The Man City subs' bench.

Manchester City

early-season fixtures for 2005–6

2 September:	Trumpton Green Primary School
9 September:	Camberwick School for the Blind
16 September:	Crimean War Veterans
23 September:	Noddy's Children's Home
30 September:	St Teresa's Home for Confused Girls
6 October:	Girl Guides (Toytown Troop)
13 October:	Boer War Amputees
20 October:	World War One Nurses' Association
27 October:	Dale Winton's All-Star XI
4 November:	St Egbert's Hospital (Lung Cancer Ward)

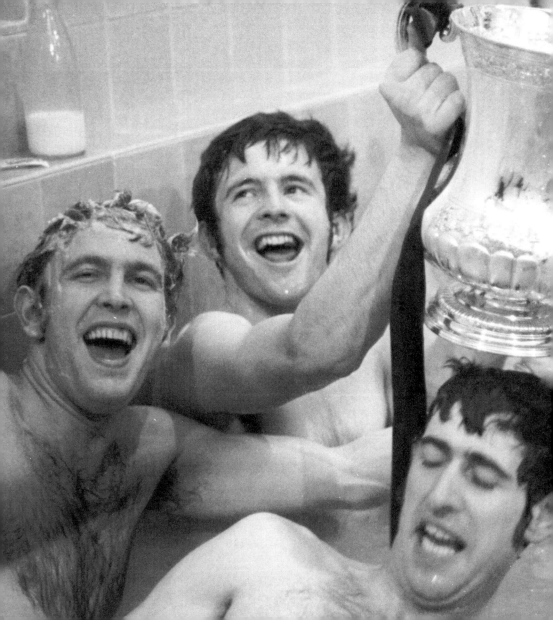

Middlesbrough

The Fire Brigade chief phones Middlesbrough's Steve McLaren in the early hours of the morning. 'Mr McLaren sir, the Riverside Stadium is on fire!' he says.

'Well, quick, get the cups, man! Save the cups! Don't stand there talking to me on the phone!' cries McLaren.

'Calm down, it's all right, Mr McLaren, the fire hasn't spread to the canteen yet.'

Middlesbrough fan: 'Hey, babe, do you want to come back to my place?'

Beautiful, intelligent woman: ' I didn't know they built toilets that big these days.'

Q: How many Middlesbrough fans does it take to screw in a lightbulb?
A: Just one, but it sure takes a shitload of lightbulbs.

The Middlesbrough Club Shop Brochure

☐ **Middlesbrough VIDEOS** – all the highlights from the last twenty years of Middlesbrough action. This ten-minute compilation, including lots of re-runs, is a perfect gift for any fan. £2.99.

☐ **Middlesbrough JOKE BOOK (vol.1)** – essential reading for all fans. This 1,600-page book is packed with some of the best jokes ever told about Boro. £12.00.

☐ **Middlesbrough BANNERS** – come complete with alphabet for making different slogans: Robson OUT, McLaren OUT, GET ME OUT OF HERE, etc. £13.00.

☐ **Middlesbrough KEEPER'S GLOVE** – essential for any fans sitting at the back of the stand. £8.99.

☐ **Middlesbrough TABLECLOTHS** – suitable for any occasion but tend to slip down the table after a brief period. £4.99.

☐ **Middlesbrough BRA** – one for the ladies. This bra, in red and white team colours, comes with good support but no cups. £1.99.

☐ **Middlesbrough LADIES' TOWELS** – the 'Mark Viduka' sanitary towel: 'In for a week, out for a month.' £1.00.

🛒 VIEW BASKET

Millwall

Q: What do you call a Millwall fan in a suit?
A: The accused.

Q: What do you call a Millwall fan in a car?
A: Arrested.

Q: What's black and brown and looks great on a Millwall fan?
A: An Alsatian.

Q: What's the difference between the Loch Ness Monster and an intelligent Millwall fan?
A: People have spotted the Loch Ness Monster.

Q: There are two Millwall fans in a car, but no pounding music. Who's driving?
A: The police.

Millwall fan: 'I'll 'ave two pints of strong lager and a packet of salt 'n' vinegar crisps, ta.'
Barman: 'Get the f**k out, scum.'

Q: What's the difference between a Millwall fan and a tree?
A: They're both w***ers apart from the tree.

Newcastle

Q: Why do Sumo wrestlers shave their legs?
A: So they don't get mistaken for Geordie women.

Q: Why do Newcastle fans plant potatoes round the edge of St James's Park?
A: So they have something to lift at the end of the season.


```
--- News report
- - - - - - - - - - - - - -
```
Newcastle have moved quickly to quash rumours of a rift between Graeme Souness and Alan Shearer. A club spokesman said: 'It's ridiculous to suggest that there is a personality clash between the two men - everybody at the club knows that Shearer hasn't got one.'

A Newcastle fan went into a shop and ordered a meal-for-one frozen dinner. As she handed over the money the check-out boy said: 'So you're single, then, are you?'

'Yes, how did you know that?' she asked.

'Because you're so ugly.'

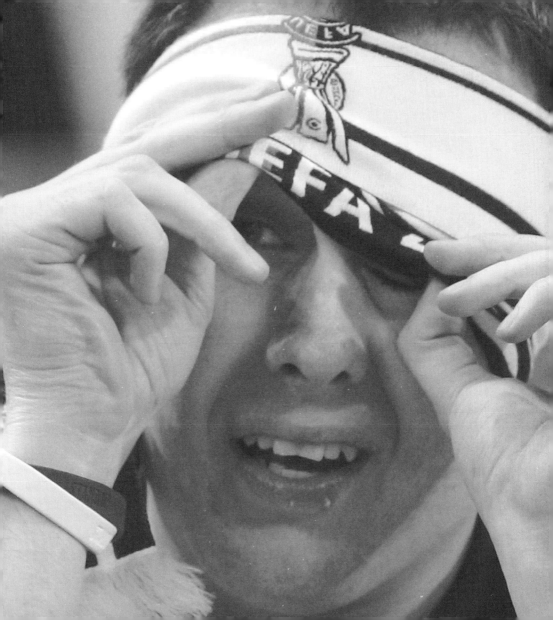

Portsmouth

Q: Why have seagulls got wings?
A: To beat Pompey fans to the rubbish tip.

Q: What is the difference between a Pompey lass and a pit bull?
A: Lipstick.

Q: Why do seagulls fly upside down in Portsmouth?
A: Because there's nothing worth shitting on.

The new Pompey manager sends scouts out around the world to look for a new striker after the ailing South Coast club has slumped to its 74th defeat on the trot. One of the scouts comes back with news of a young Iraqi striker, who he is convinced will turn out to be a legend in the game. The Pompey manager flies to Baghdad to see him in action. He is highly impressed and snaps up the young lad in a five-year deal.

A week later, Pompey are 4–0 down to Man United with just twenty minutes left when the manager decides to give the young Iraqi his first taste of Premiership action. The boy takes the match by storm, scoring five goals in the final fifteen minutes to seal a remarkable win. Fratton Park erupts with delight at the final whistle as the young Iraqi runs off the pitch to phone his mum and tell her about his incredible first day in English football.

'Hi, Mum, you'll never guess,' he says. 'I played for twenty minutes today, we were 4–0 down but I scored five and we won the game. Everybody loves me: the fans, the press, the players, the coaches … It's great.'

'Well, I'm glad one of us had a good day,' replies his mum bitterly. 'Let me tell you about my day. Your father got shot dead in the street, your sister got raped, I was ambushed and beaten by a band of looters, your brother has become a gangster, there is raw sewage running in the streets, and we can't sleep for the sound of gunfire and the wailing of police cars and ambulances …'

The young Iraqi is very upset. 'I'm so sorry, Mum.'

'How we let you persuade us to move to Portsmouth in the first place, I'll never know.'

Sheffield United

Sheffield girl: 'Mum, why are your hands so soft?'
Mum: 'Because I'm twelve.'

A Sheffield United fan goes to the council to register for child benefit.

'How many children?' asks the council worker.

'Ten,' replies the girl.

'Wow, ten?' says the council worker. 'Can you give me their names?'

'Wayne, Wayne, Wayne, Wayne, Wayne, Wayne, Wayne, Wayne, Wayne and Wayne.'

'Doesn't that ever get confusing?'

'Naah,' says the girl. 'It's great because if they are out playing in the street I just have to shout: "WAAAYNE, YER TEA'S READY!!" or "WAAAYNE, OFF TO SCHOOL NOW!!" And they all do it.'

'What if you want to speak to one of them individually?' says the council worker.

'That's easy, too,' says the girl. 'I just use their surnames.'

The Saints

SOUTHAMPTON v ARSENAL

Saturday 19th May 2001 Kick-off 3.00pm

SOUTHAMPTON v ARSENAL
SATURDAY 19TH MAY 2001 KICK OFF 3.00pm

TODAY'S OFFICIALS
REFEREE
P. Taylor
ASSISTANT REFEREES
M.J. Cairns
M.S. Yerby

Southampton

Two Southampton fans are walking down the road to St Mary's stadium when they spot an advert in a chemist's window, saying: 'Free Saints Season Tickets. Apply Within.'

One of them heads into the shop while the other waits outside.

A full half-hour later the man comes back out of the shop and hands his mate a packet of ribbed, curry-flavoured condoms and a massive double-ended vibrator.

'What the hell's all this? Where are the season tickets?' asks his mate.

'Sorry, in the end I was just too embarrassed to ask.'

A Southampton boy turns to his father after the match and asks:
'How many points do we have, Daddy?'

'Fifteen points, little Johnny,' comes the reply.

'Right, so where's my Easter eggs, then?'

Sunderland

Q: How many Sunderland fans does it take to change a lightbulb?
A: Yeah, right, like they've got electricity in Sunderland.

Q: What do you say to a Sunderland supporter with a good-looking bird on his arm?
A: Nice tattoo.


```
--- News report
---------------
```
A new red and white Oxo Cube will be introduced early next year. It will be called 'Laughing Stock'.

Q: What's long, smelly, and goes around corners in Sunderland?
A: The dole queue.

A Sunderland fan takes his son to the Stadium of Light and at the turnstile he hands over thirty quid and says: 'Two, please.'

'Would that be forwards or midfielders?' the operator replies.

Swansea

The most popular car sticker in Swansea: 'A dog is for life, not just for the honeymoon.'

A Swansea fan, depressed by his appearance, goes to see his psychiatrist. 'Doctor, I feel so low. I have no friends, no social life, people look away when I walk into the room, and some even cross the street as I walk towards them. Is there any way you can help me come to terms with my severe ugliness and allow me to grow in confidence?'

'Of course,' says the psychiatrist. 'Just pop yourself on the couch and lie face-down.'

Q: How do you find the cathedral in the city of Swansea?
A: Get off the Metro in Swansea, go past the international art gallery, turn right at the Bill Gates business centre and follow the signs for Swansea international airport. When you see the state-of-the-art Swansea Arena, park your car in the television station car park, take a short cut through the field full of elves and pixies, past the lake full of mermaids, stopping only to feed the dodos on the way …

Tottenham

Q: What's the difference between Tottenham Hotspur and a good w**k?
A: You can't beat a good w**k.

Q: Why did Tottenham go on the stock exchange?
A: To prove that crap can float.

Q: What's the difference between a busload of Tottenham fans and a hedgehog?
A: On a hedgehog, the pricks are on the outside.

Tottenham Hotspur helpline:

0800-won-nothing-won-nothing-won-nothing.

Following the fall of Saddam Hussein's regime, former Iraqi Information Minister Mohammed Saeed Al-Sahaf, aka 'Comical Ali', has been appointed the new spokesman for Tottenham Hotspur. Below are the main points from his first press briefing with the great North London club:

'We are enjoying yet another tremendous season. We look forward to lifting the Premiership trophy once again as we continue to demolish and humiliate our pathetic foes.'

'Our players are the fastest, strongest, bravest and most skilled in the world. Their biggest danger is falling asleep during matches as they are bored by the lack of a proper fight.'

'Our manager is a strategic genius and a wonderful man who the whole country loves with all their heart.'

'Our youth development is so good our under-ten off-games girls' team could beat Brazil to win the World Cup without any difficulty.'

'Tottenham fans are the most intelligent, charming, humble fans in Britain. Any one of them could become a top international manager tomorrow, or a leading diplomat, if the wish took him.'

'Our endless sequence of triumphs over the infidel Arsenal will continue to be brutal and unresisted. We will never beat our scumdog rivals by fewer than fifteen goals.'

West Bromwich Albion

Q: What does Bryan Robson say when West Brom score a goal?
A: Good work, boys. Now let's try to get a goal at the other end of the pitch.'

West Brom were widely predicted to stay in the Premiership for three whole seasons: **Autumn, Winter and Spring.**

West Ham

Q: What's the first question at a West Ham quiz night?
A: Wot u f**kin' lookin' at?

A family of West Ham fans attend a wedding at which the bride is marrying an officer of the Royal Navy. As the happy couple leave the church they walk through a traditional arch of twelve rowing sculls held by the groom's shipmates.

'Luv a duck, look at all vose gorgeous sailors and all vem oars,' says the young girl of the family.

'Them ain't 'ores, love,' says her father. 'They're the effing bridesmaids.'

Q: How many West Ham fans does it take to change a lightbulb?
A: Three. One to change the bulb, one to be a witness and the third to shoot the witness.

Q: What do you get if you see a West Ham fan buried up to his neck in sand?
A: More sand.

Wolverhampton Wanderers

A Wolves supporter goes to his doctor to find out what's wrong with him.
  'Your problem is that you're fat,' the doctor tells him.
  'Well, I'd like a second opinion,' replies the Wolves fan.
  'OK, you're ugly and you stink, too.'

General

Michael Owen heads into a nightclub, goes straight up to a woman and starts feeling her tits. 'Get your coat, love, you're coming home with me,' he says.

'You're a little forward, aren't you?' replies the woman.

David Beckham decides to go out horseriding one day, even though he has never had any lessons. He jumps on to the steed's back in one bound, as though he has been riding all his life, and the horse immediately leaps into motion. It moves along at a steady pace as Posh stands back in admiration, but then David slowly begins to slip from the saddle as the pace of the beast quickens. In sheer terror David grabs the horse's mane but he struggles to get a firm grip. He makes a desperate lunge to throw his arms around the horse's neck but he ends up sliding further down the side of the horse. The horse just gallops along, apparently oblivious to the blood-curdling shrieks of its rider. Finally, David loses his fingertip hold and, as he tries to make a jump to safety, his foot gets stuck in the stirrup irons, and he plunges earthwards and his head begins to bounce up and down on the ground. Posh can only watch helplessly as her husband's head is smashed repeatedly against the ground. He is just seconds from losing consciousness when the Tesco's trolley collector sees what is happening, reaches over and unplugs the horse.

David Beckham is running around his mansion shouting joyfully: 'Forty-fwee days, Vic. Just forty-fwee days! Wow!'

Posh asks him why he's so happy.

'Well, honey-buns, I've finished this Thomas the Tank Engine jigsaw in just forty-fwee days!'

'And that's good, is it?' asks Posh.

'Good? Good?' replies David in disbelief. 'It says three to six years on the box!'

BBC football pundit Gary Lineker conducts a double-headed interview with managers Peter Reid and Sam Allardyce. He turns to Reid first, asking: 'So, Peter, what are your hopes for your team this season?'

'Well, if we can pick up a few points here and there, scrap a result every now and then, hopefully we'll still be in the top flight come the end of the season.'

Gary then asks Allardyce the same question, and Big Sam replies: 'Well, we'll walk the Premiership, pick up the League Cup and FA Cup along the way, and then we'll round off the season by winning the Champions League to be crowned Kings of Europe.'

Lineker raises a quizzical eyebrow before saying: 'Erm, Sam, don't you think you're being just a little bit overambitious there?'

'Well, Peter bloody started it!' replies Sam.

Carlton Palmer went to Cinderella's party as a pumpkin, but come midnight he still hadn't turned into a coach.

David Beckham is convinced that Posh has been having an affair and he is beside himself with rage. In his fury, he rushes out and buys a gun before returning home to confront his wife, only to find her in bed with none other than his England colleague Wayne Rooney.

Beckham is doubly appalled that his wife should have fallen for the man known as Shrek to his team mates, and he points the gun at his own head.

'No, David, don't do it!' Posh screams as she jumps off the bed. 'I'm sorry, David. I'm sure we can work this out.'

'Shut up and back off, Victorwia,' Beckham snaps. 'You're next.'

Why did the chicken cross the road?
The managers give their version of events …

Arsène Wenger:
'From where I was sitting in the dugout I did not see the incident clearly so I would not like to comment. But I have to say it is obvious that he gets picked on by opposition players and fans every game. Perhaps people in England are a bit chicken-o-phobic.'

David O'Leary:
'To be fair to the lad, he's just a baby chick really, and crossing the road is something that will come with experience. He's a lovely lad, and he'll learn from the experience, but I don't seriously expect him to cross it this season. The money's not there just to go out and buy a load of experienced chickens. The board have told me that if I want a chicken with loads of road-crossing experience under his belt, then I'll have to sell some of the others first. But I won't be doing that. They're only young 'uns.'

Peter Reid:
'No excuses – the f**king useless chicken f**k should've just f**king got on with it, crossed the f**king road without f**king moaning and taken it on the f**king chin and just f**king put it behind him. And you can f**k off as well.'

Glenn Hoddle:
'At the end of the day, the chicken was hit by the
dustcart when crossing the road because in a
previous life it had been a bad chicken. At the end of
the day the fella didn't have his clever hat on today.'

Sven Goran Eriksson:
'For sure, of course, he's a chicken. A good chicken and, yes, for sure, he
has a chance of crossing the road, just like all the other chickens. You
have many good chickens in this country.'

Jose Mourinho:
'For me, I don't care what people think of my views of the chicken. If they
think I'm arrogant, then, OK, I can take that. Yeah, the chicken's OK, sure,
but what do want me to say? That he's the best chicken in the whole of
Europe? Well, if the chicken parks his bus right in front of our goal, to my
mind that is not crossing the road. And, besides, at half-time I saw the
chicken going into the referee's office for a quiet chat. I don't care what
you think.'

Kevin Keegan:
'Yeah, OK, hands up, the chicken's dead; but, hey, you know, I still feel
that not long from now he can go all the way to the other side of the road.
This was just one of those days when things didn't go for the lad. But hey.'

Bryan Robson is queuing in his local building society when a gunman bursts in through the door demanding money. Robbo attempts to tackle the raider, but gets knocked over, and as he falls he smashes his head on the counter and is out cold. The robber escapes, and the cashier tries to revive Robson. After a few minutes he comes round and looks bewildered. His first words are: 'Where the hell am I?'

'Don't worry, it's OK, you're in the Nationwide, Mr Robson,' says the cashier.

'F**k me, is it May already?' replies Robson.

--- News report
- - - - - - - - - - - - - -

Peter Reid was caught speeding on his way to the training ground yesterday. 'I'll do anything for three points,' he told police.

Q: When did Martin Keown's mum start to get morning sickness?
A: The day after he was born.

Q: When did Ivan Campo realize he was never going to be a male model?
A: When a dog started humping his leg with its eyes closed.

Tributes have been pouring in from all over the football world following the news that Blackpool, Stoke and England great Sir Stanley Matthews passed away in the night.

Pele described him as 'a sublime talent and a wonderful ambassador'.

Bobby Charlton said he was 'the best player ever to pull on an England shirt'.

Kevin Keegan said he was 'a once-in-a-lifetime legend'.

David Beckham said: 'It's really upsetting because Posh and I have always loved his Turkey Twizzlers. They're bootiful. He will be sorely missed in our house.'

David Beckham goes shopping in a department store and, spotting a Thermos flask on the shelf, he says to an assistant: 'What the hell is that weird thing for?'

'It's to keep hot things hot and cold things cold, Mr Beckham,' says the girl.

Beckham is impressed, buys one and takes it home to show it off to Posh before taking it to England training the following day.

'For sure, what have you got there, David?' asks Sven Goran Eriksson.

'It's to keep hot things hot and cold things cold,' says David.

'Excellent,' says Sven. 'What have you got in it?'

'Hot chocolate and some ice cream.'

A MASSIVE EARTHQUAKE MEASURING 2.2 ON THE RICHTER SCALE HAS STRUCK THE NORTH OF ENGLAND. ITS EPICENTRE WAS MANCHESTER.

The earthquake destroyed the entire Greater Manchester area, causing over 500 pounds' worth of damage. Six boroughs of historic litter and slum interest were razed to the ground. Hundreds of thousands were shaken awake long before their giro arrived. Shortly after the quake struck, victims could be seen wandering the streets aimlessly muttering: 'Sorted ... 'Ar kid ... Cum on, then ...' Experts believe that it will be years before the shocked community comes to terms with the fact that something remotely interesting has happened in Manchester.

One resident, Shazza Dirtbag, a fifteen-year-old single mother of three, said: 'It was a terrible shock. My littlest, Chardonnay-Waynetta, was still crying when I was trying to watch Kilroy this morning.'

Looting across the city, however, did carry on as normal, police said.

The British Red Cross responded immediately to the humanitarian crisis by shipping 3,000 crates of cheap lager, 4,000 crates of Sunny Delight and 5,000 buckets of KFC to the area. Rescue workers sifting through the rubble have recovered vast amounts of personal belongings, including Social Security benefit books, guns, bags of crack and shell-suits.

Within hours the government had launched a worldwide Manchester Earthquake Appeal and said it expected to raise at least £4.50 by the end of the week.

What your donated money will buy:

20p: A biro for filling in dodgy compensation and incapacity benefits claims.

£2.00: A bag of chips, ten Superkings, and a bottle of fake Coke for a family of five.

£3.00: A new house in an upmarket area for a family of five.

Matt Le Tissier was so ugly that when he was a baby his mother left him outside and called the police and then went and handed herself in.

Roy Carroll is so distraught after his latest blunder that he decides to end it all. He walks straight out of Old Trafford and throws himself down in front of a number 12 bus. Luckily, it passes right under him.

Q: Why do Brazilians make great lovers?
A: Because they can lob Seaman from fifty yards.
(Reference to long-range effort by Ronaldinho in 2002 World Cup quarter-final.)

Two friends are on the bus going to the match, and as they approach the traffic lights they notice a long funeral procession coming in the opposite direction. One of them immediately takes off his hat, closes his eyes and bows his head in prayer. The other says: 'Blimey, that is the most thoughtful and lovely gesture I have ever seen. You truly are a kind man.'
 'Well, we were married thirty-five years.'

Bryan Robson is wheeling his shopping trolley across the supermarket car park when he notices an old lady struggling with her bags of shopping. He stops and asks her: 'Can you manage, dear?'
 To which the old lady replies: 'F**k off. You got yourself into this mess; don't ask me to sort it out.'

England goalkeeper David James is out shopping for new hair products one day when he hears desperate screams from a nearby building. He looks up to see plumes of dark smoke billowing from a fifth-storey window, with a woman leaning out holding a baby.

'Help me!' she screams. 'Please, someone, catch my baby!'

James runs through the crowd and shouts: 'You're all right, love, I'm the Manchester City and England goalkeeper. I'm famous for my safe hands. Drop the baby. I promise I'll catch her.' He takes the goalkeeper's stance with his legs apart, slightly bent at the knees, and his arms stretched outwards.

'OK!' screams the woman. 'I've no choice! Here goes.' With the flames closing in on her, the woman lets go of her baby, but its blanket catches on the window and the tot flies off at an angle, tumbling head over heels as she speeds towards the ground.

The mother screams, and the crowd holds its breath, convinced the babe is just seconds from death.

James appears frozen to the spot, but when the spinning baby is just feet from the ground James leaps an amazing twenty feet across the pavement, catches the child in his giant hands and pulls her safely in towards his chest.

The crowd erupts in delight, and the mother immediately weeps with relief. Still holding the child to his chest, James waves to the crowd of onlookers to acknowledge their applause. Then, slowly and gracefully, he turns away from them, bounces the baby twice on the ground, and dropkicks her seventy yards down the road.

One morning Wayne Rooney rushes into the local surgery to see his doctor, looking deeply disturbed.

'Doctor, you have to take a look at me immediately,' Wayne blurts. 'When I woke up today, I looked at myself in the mirror and my hair was all manky, my skin was all spotty and pasty, my eyes were bloodshot and sticking out. I looked like puke warmed up. What on earth is wrong with me, Doc?'

The doctor looks the Man United and England star over for a couple of minutes before saying: 'Well, I can tell you for starters that there's nothing wrong with your eyesight, that's for sure.'

A City and United fan collide in a huge accident on the motorway. Their cars are a wreck, but both men walk way unhurt.

'This must be a sign from above that we are meant to be friends after all,' says the City fan.

'I think you're right,' says the United fan.

The City fan then returns to his wrecked car and takes a bottle of malt whisky from the back seat. 'Here,' he says to the United fan, 'let's drink to our miraculous survival and new friendship.'

He passes the bottle over to the United fan, who takes a huge gulp from the bottle to steady his nerves before passing it back to the City fan, who promptly pops it back in his car.

'Aren't you having any?' asks the United fan.

'No,' replies the City fan. 'I think I'll wait till the police get here.'

Christmas Cracker Factory

Football's Worst Jokes

Q: What would David Beckham's name be if he was a Spice Girl?
A: Waste of Spice.

Q: Why do Rangers fans never cross the road?
A: Because they are waiting for the green man to turn orange.

Q: Why does Bryan Robson keep visiting Argos?
A: Because that's the only way he can pick up any Premier points.

Q: What tea do footballers drink?
A. PenalTea.

Q: What do goalkeepers have for their tea?
A: Beans on post.

Q: What do you call a laughing footballer?
A: Ryan Giggles.

Q: What part of a football pitch smells nicest?
A: The scenter spot.

Q: What's the chilliest ground in the Premiership?
A: Cold Trafford.

Q: How did the football pitch end up a triangle?
A: Somebody took a corner.

Q: Which famous player keeps up the fuel supply?
A: Paul gas coin.

Q: What does Paul Ince's mum make for Christmas?
A: Ince pies.

Q: What do a footballer and a magician have in common?
A: Both do hat tricks.

Q: Which goalkeeper can jump higher than a crossbar?
A: All of them – a crossbar can't jump.

Q: Why are football players never asked to dinner?
A: Because they're always dribbling.

Q: Why did the footballer hold his boot to his ear?
A: Because he liked sole music.

Arsène Wenger: 'Our new winger cost five million pounds. I call him our wonder player.
Sir Alex Ferguson: 'Why's that?'
Wenger: 'Because every time he plays I wonder why I bothered to buy him!'

Q: Why will England never win the World Cup?
A: They keep scoring Owen goals.

Q: What's the difference between Pamela Anderson and the Liverpool goal?
A: Pam's only got two tits in front of her.

Q: What have General Pinochet and Tottenham Hotspur got in common?
A: They both round people up into football stadiums and torture them.

Elland Road boss Peter Ridsdale has sacked David Leary and employed a new Chinese manager. His name: Win One Soon.

Q: Why did a footballer take a piece of rope on to the pitch?
A: He was the skipper.

Q: What lights up a football stadium?
A: A football match.

Q: What is the bank manager's favourite type of football?
A: Fiver side.


```
--- News report
- - - - - - - - - - - - - -
```
Newcastle football club are under investigation by the Inland Revenue for tax evasion. They've been claiming for silver polish for the past thirty years.

Q: What's the difference between Tottenham and an albatross?
A: An albatross has got two decent wings.

Q: What's the difference between Coventry City and the Bermuda Triangle?
A: The Bermuda Triangle has three points.

Q: Which part of a football stadium is never the same from one day to the next?
A: The changing rooms.

Q: Which team loves ice-cream?
A: Aston Vanilla.

Q: What should a team do if the pitch is flooded?
A: Bring on their subs.

Referee

A ventriloquist on a nationwide tour of football clubs is appearing at a function in the club bar of a small town. He's going through his usual run of stupid-referee jokes when a referee stands up at the back of the room and splutters: 'I've had quite enough of your pathetic referee jokes! You're just stereotyping us all as blind buffoons with the brains of a gerbil. It's people like you who keep good, honest people like me from being respected in the workplace, in my local community and by the football fans of this country!' The ventriloquist is clearly embarrassed by this tirade and starts to stutter an apology, but the referee interrupts him, saying: 'Stay out of this, mate, I'm talking to the little bugger on your knee!'

Hours after the end of the world, a border dispute erupts between Heaven and Hell. God holds talks with the Devil to find a way to resolve the dispute, and Satan suggests a football game between the two eternal communities to settle the issue.

'The heat down there must be affecting your brain,' says God. 'Don't you know all the good players go to heaven?'

'That may be, but we've got all the refs,' replies the Devil.

First man: 'We're starting up an amateur football team. Would you care to join?'

Second man (with dribble on his chin): 'I would love to, but I'm afraid I don't know the first thing about football.'

First man: 'Don't worry, we could do with a referee as well.'

A referee goes into a sports shop and asks the sales assistant: 'Do you have any referee kit?'

The assistant says: 'Sorry, I'm afraid we don't stock any.'

The referee holds his chin and thinks for a moment before continuing: 'Well, can I have a wasp instead, please?'

'A wasp? What do you mean, a wasp? This is a sports shop, for heaven's sake.'

'Well, you had one in the window yesterday.'

A referee and a linesman are walking down the street. The referee says: 'Gosh, look at that poor dead bird.' The linesman immediately looks up into the sky and says: 'Where?'

The captain was angry with a decision against his team and confronted the referee. 'What would happen if I called you a useless blind bastard with the brains of a Yorkshire terrier?'

'Well, I would show you a red card.'

'And what if I just thought it?'

'So long as you don't say anything, there's nothing I can do.'

'Well, let's leave it like that, shall we?' says the captain.

Referee: 'Doctor, Doctor, I think I need my eyes tested.'
Man: 'You certainly do, sir. You're in a fish and chip shop.

Q: How can you tell when a referee has sent you a fax?
A: Because it has a stamp on it.

Q: Why did the referee keep checking his letterbox?
A: Because his computer kept telling him he had mail.

Q: What do you see when you look deep into a referee's eyes?

A: The back of his head.

Q: How do you change a referee's mind?
A: Blow in his ear.

Q: How do you keep a referee busy all day?
A: Give him a piece of paper with 'Please Turn Over' written on both sides.

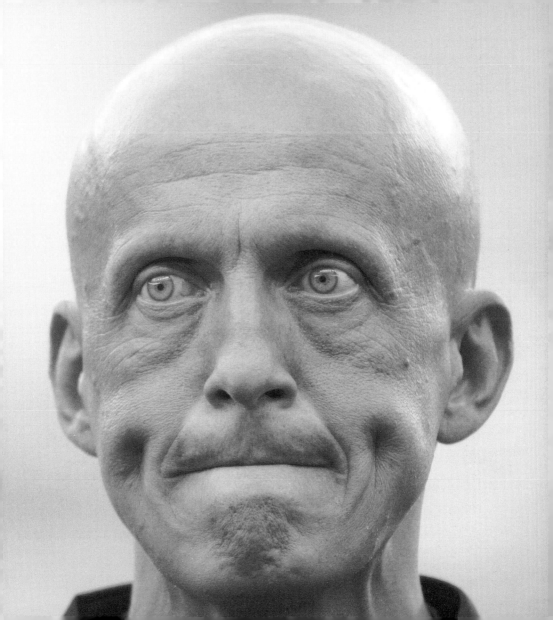

Q: Why did the chicken run on to the football pitch?
A: Because the ref called a foul.

Q: How do you sink a submarine full of referees?
A: Knock on the hatch.

Q: How do you confuse a referee?
A: You don't. They're just born that way.

After a match a hungry referee walks into a library, goes up to the counter and says: 'Cod and chips, large, with a side order of mushy peas and a pickled egg, please.'

'But this is a library,' says the bemused librarian.

So the referee leans forward and whispers softly: 'Sorry about that. Can I have cod and chips, large, with a side order of mushy peas and a pickled egg, please.'

Q: How can you tell when you have a serious acne problem?
A: Referees start reading your face.

Q: How do you spot a referee on a nudists' beach?
A: He hasn't got an erection.

Q: How does a sky-diving referee know he's about to reach the ground?
A: His guide dog's lead goes slack.

A referee goes to the doctor, who tells him he needs to get glasses.

'But you haven't even examined me yet,' protests the referee.

'I don't need to. I knew it from the moment you walked in through the window.'

After a gruelling game that has gone to extra time, a referee staggers into the physiotherapist's room in the tunnel. 'Blimey, I'm hurting all over. I just don't know what the hell I've done to myself out there.'

'What do you mean, you hurt all over?

'Look, I'll show you,' says the ref. He proceeds to touch his leg. 'Ouch!' he shouts. Then he touches his earlobe. 'Ouch again!' Then he touches his hair. 'Ouch! Even my hair hurts!' he screams.

The physio doesn't even bother to examine him, but says: 'Ref, you have a broken finger.'

An assistant referee turns up for a game with both his ears bandaged up.

'What happened to your ears?' asks the referee.

The assistant referee replies: 'Yesterday I was ironing my linesman's flag when the phone rang and I answered the iron by mistake.'

'That explains one ear, but what happened to the other one?' asks the referee.

'Well, I had to call the doctor, stupid!' says the assistant referee.

Q: Why are the referee's legs always wet?
A: Because his guide dog's blind, too.

One day there is an explosion at the mine where the seven dwarfs are working. When they don't arrive home for their dinner at the usual time, Snow White goes to investigate. When she realizes what has happened she calls down the mineshaft and hears a faint voice, muttering: 'I want to be a referee … I want to be a referee …'

'Well, at least Dopey's still alive,' Snow White says to herself.

Manchester United

Q: How many Manchester United fans does it take to change a lightbulb?

A: Three. One to change the bulb, one to buy the souvenir T-shirt and video, and one to drive the other two back to Guildford.

Q: What has Old Trafford at ten to five on a Saturday afternoon got in common with Wormwood Scrubs prison?

A: They are both full of cockneys trying to get out.

Q: What was the hardest six years of Wayne Rooney's life?

A: Class One at primary school.

Q: What's the difference between a dead dog in the road and a dead Man United fan?

A: There are skid marks in front of the dog.

Q: Why can't you get a cup of tea at Old Trafford?

A: All the mugs are on the field and all the cups are at Highbury.

Q: What's the difference between a Man United fan and a dildo?

A: A Man United fan is a real prick.

Manchester United Computer Viruses Explained

The Manchester United fan virus. Your computer develops a memory disorder and deletes information about the football world pre-1993.

The Manchester United shirt virus. Tough one to detect as it changes format every three months.

The David Beckham virus. The computer looks great, all the lights are on but nothing inside works. (This virus has been eliminated in England, but after resurfacing in Spain for a short while there are fears it may make a return.)

The Roy Keane virus (aka The Alan Smith virus). Kicks you out of windows.

The Sir Alex Ferguson virus. The computer develops a horrible whining noise. The on-screen clock runs slower than all the other computers in England, and tends to blow fuses when under small amounts of pressure.

The Ryan Giggs virus. The computer thinks it's more intelligent than it actually is, and also causes dramatic fluctuations in performance.

The Roy Carroll virus. The computer looks perfectly normal but it can't save anything.

The Ruud Van Nistelrooy virus. This is a problem that began in Holland before spreading to England – images of what appears to be the lovechild of Shergar and Hugh Grant start flashing up and down on your screen.

The Paul Scholes virus. Curious one, this. The computer turns ginger, and its little willy keeps popping out.

Q: Can you list three English football clubs with a rude word in their name?
A: Arsenal, Scunthorpe and f**king Manchester United.

Q: What's the difference between Sir Alex Ferguson and God?
A: God doesn't think he's Sir Alex Ferguson.

Q: Why does Phil Neville throw bread down the loo?
A: To feed the toilet duck.

Q: How can you tell that Roy Keane has been using the computer?
A: There's Tippex all over the screen.

'You are so bloody stupid,' shouts Sir Alex Ferguson at Phil Neville during a training session. 'I'm going to ask you a very basic question and if you get it wrong I'll have to consider you too thick to play against Real Madrid on Saturday. We need intelligent players against that cunning lot. OK, so what's two plus two?'

'Is it four, boss?' replies Neville.

Before Fergie has a chance to reply, the rest of the team shout as one: 'That's a bit harsh, gaffer. Give him an easier one to start with.'

Keane, Giggs and Scholes are heading into training one afternoon when the little ginger one says: 'Hey, why don't we bunk off? The gaffer leaves at midday on Wednesdays. He'll never bloody know!'

So they all make a run for it back to their sports cars and drive home. When Scholes walks in the front door he sees Fergie's bare arse bouncing up and down and his wife screaming with pleasure as the pair of them writhe around on the hall floor.

The following Wednesday, Keano suggests they all skive off again as it was such a success. Giggsy's up for it, too, but Scholesy goes: 'No chance, lads; I almost got caught last week.'

Sir Alex Ferguson is sitting at home one morning when the phone rings. It's team captain Roy Keane and he is sounding a little agitated.

'What's up, Roy my lad?' asks Sir Alex.

'Well, gaffer, my wife gave me a jigsaw to do to help me relax between games, but it's doing my head in because none of the pieces fit together. It's bloody impossible, boss.'

'I certainly don't want this distracting you before Saturday's big game against those London bastards, so bring it round and I'll see if I can help.'

Ten minutes later Keano turns up at Ferguson's house with the puzzle under his arm. Ferguson ushers him through to the kitchen, where Roy empties the pieces on to the table. Ferguson looks down in dismay before turning to his inspirational midfielder and saying: 'Now, Roy, just put the f**king Frosties back in the box, will you?'

Q: What is the difference between Sir Alex Ferguson and a jet engine?
A: The jet engine will eventually stop whining.

Wayne Rooney walks into a fish and chip shop and orders a large chips and a piece of fish. The man behind the counter says: 'It won't be long, Mr Rooney.'

'Well, it better be a nice fat one, then,' says Wayne.

Have you heard the one about the Manchester United player who spent three weeks studying for his urine test?

Sir Alex Ferguson walks into Manchester United's training centre one morning and finds Wayne Rooney staring at a carton of orange juice.

'What in Rob Roy's name do you think you are doing, my lad?' asks the Scot.

'It says concentrate, boss,' replies Wayne.

Q: What's the difference between listening to Sir Alex Ferguson's after-match interview and childbirth?
A: One's an extremely painful, frightening experience, and the other's just having a baby.

A Man United fan dies on match day and goes to heaven in his Man United shirt. He knocks on the old pearly gates, and out walks St Peter, who takes one look at the new arrival and says: 'Sorry, no Man United fans in heaven.'

'But I've been really good all my life,' protests the Man United supporter.

'Yeah, right,' says St Peter. 'What have you done that's so good, then?'

'Well, to give you some recent examples, three weeks before I died I gave a hundred pounds to the starving children of Africa.'

'And?' says St Peter.

'Well, two weeks before I died I gave a hundred pounds to the homeless of Salford.'

'Keep going.'

'Last week I gave a hundred pounds to the Save the Planet fund.'

'All right,' says St Peter, 'wait here a second while I have a quick word with the gaffer.'

St Peter returns ten minutes later and says to the anxious-looking Man United fan: 'I've had a word with the Almighty and we are at one on this. Here's your three hundred quid back. Now f**k off.'

Phil Neville wakes up one morning and hears the dustbin men doing their rounds. He quickly jumps out of bed, scrambling over his *Beano* comics. Running into the drive he shouts to one of the dustmen: 'Am I too late for the rubbish?'

'No!' comes the reply. 'Jump in.'

The Man United players are in the dressing room on Saturday not long before kick-off when Roy Keane walks in with a furrowed brow.

'Boss,' he says, 'there's a problem. I'm not playing unless I get a cortisone injection.'

'Hey, that's not fair,' pipes Rio Ferdinand. 'If he's having a new car, so am I.'

Ryan Giggs walks into training with a pile of dog crap in his hand and says to Sir Alex Ferguson: 'Hey, gaffer, look what I nearly trod in.'

Two Man United fans are walking down the street at five o'clock on a Saturday evening.

First Man United fan: 'I couldn't make the game at Old Trafford today, I was at a funeral. What was the score?'

Second Man United fan: 'We drew 0–0.'

First Man United fan: 'Who missed our penalty?'

Q: What is Gary Neville's best position?
A: Drawback.

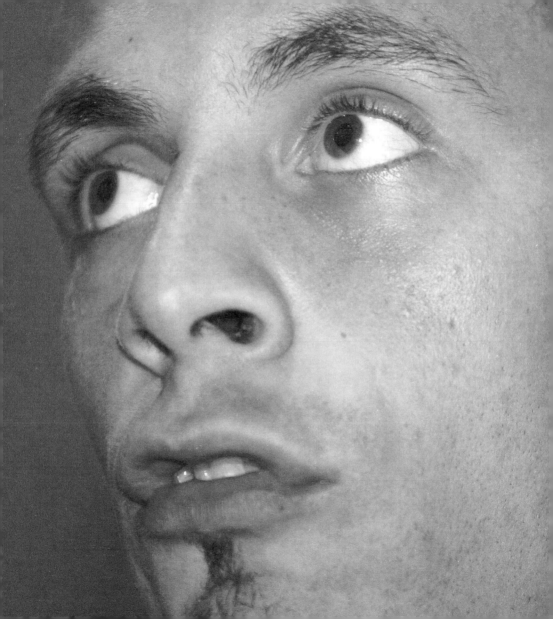

As part of the Government's campaign to improve Maths standards in England's primary schools, it has published **The Official Man United Maths Workbook**. Below is a sample test paper from the new book:

1. Roy is 82 yards away from the referee at Old Trafford and Gary is 71 yards away. If Roy can run at 20mph and Gary at 16mph, who will be sticking their eye-popping, vein-bulging head into the referee's face first, assuming Roy does not stop to head-butt an opponent on his way, and Gary doesn't trip over himself?

2. Ryan is from Wales. Express, as a percentage, the number of internationals he has missed on a Wednesday through injury only to have made a remarkable recovery for a club match on Saturday.

3. If one minute of time has been taken up by treatment for injuries in the second half of a given match at Old Trafford, how much injury time will be added on by the referee if Man United are losing? Round your answer to the nearest five minutes.

4. You are the referee at Old Trafford. How close to a visiting defender does Ruud van Nistelrooy need to be for the Dutchman to earn a penalty when he goes down in the penalty area as if he has just been taken out by a sniper? Round your answer to the nearest ten metres.

5. Phil Neville has fifty international caps. If you take away the number of appearances when he was the only adult male in England who could just about kick the ball with his left foot, how many are left?

6. Graham 'The Red Devil' lives in Guildford. How much does it cost for him and his two sons to travel to the Theatre of Nightmares every other weekend, including souvenir matchday programme, a few drinks and a stack of prawn sandwiches? How much could he save per week if he watched his local team instead? Round your answer to the nearest thousand pounds.

7. Manchester United are regarded as the giants of world football. How many more European Cup finals have they appeared in than Steaua Bucharest?

8. Sir Alex has won it once. Bob has won in three times. Sir Alex has one, Bob has none. What does Sir Alex have?

9. What is the total number of chickens counted before they were hatched by Manchester United and their supporters before the start of the season?

Filthy

Q: What do Cardiff girls do for foreplay?
A: Get their coats.

Q: What do Newcastle girls do on Saturday morning?
A: Introduce themselves.

Q: Why do Sunderland girls have orgasms?
A: So they know when to stop having sex.

Q: Why is David Beckham like a Ferrero Rocher?
A: They both come in a posh box.

Q: What do you give the Liverpool girl that has everything?
A: Penicillin.

Q: What do David Beckham and British Rail trains have in common?
A: They both go in and out of Victoria.

There's speculation in the City that after their Northern Rock sponsorship deal expires Newcastle United will team up with a new sponsor – Tampax. The United board thought it was an appropriate change as the club is going through a very bad period.

Q: What's the difference between a Newcastle lass and a Kit-Kat?
A: You only get four fingers in a Kit-Kat.

Q: What does the Middlesbrough girl say after having sex?
A: 'So who are you guys playing next week?'

Q: Why do Sunderland girls wear knickers?
A: To keep their ankles warm.

Q: How can you tell when a Sunderland lass is having an orgasm?
A: She drops her chips.

Q: What does a Colchester girl use for protection when having sex?
A: A bus shelter.

Q: How does a Liverpool lass turn on the light after sex?
A: She opens the car door.

Q: What do Newcastle girls put behind their ears to attract men?
A: Their ankles.

Q: What's the difference between Sunderland girls and the House of Lords?
A: Only a few people have entered the Lords.

Q: What's Scouse for foreplay?
A: 'Are you awake, luv?'

Q: What's Yorkshire for foreplay?
A: 'Are you awake, Mum?'

Q: What's Welsh for foreplay?
A: 'Baaaa.'

Q: Why do Birmingham girls prefer cars with sun roofs?
A: Because they get more leg-room.

Q: Why do Gillingham girls wear big-hooped earrings?
A: So they have somewhere to rest their legs.

Blackburn girl: 'Mum, I have been out with ten blokes in the last few weeks and I haven't let one of them shag me.'
Mum: 'What was wrong with him?'

A Newcastle girl goes to confession and says to the priest: 'Father, I slept with twelve blokes last night.'
Priest: 'Well, after saying four Hail Marys, go home and eat twelve onions.
Newcastle girl: 'Twelve onions. Why?'
Priest: 'Because that will help wipe the smile off your face.'

Q: How does a Plymouth girl get rid of excess pubic hair?
A: She spits it out.

A player goes down under a heavy tackle and is writhing in pain as the female physiotherapist runs on to the pitch. 'Don't worry,' she says. 'I can reduce the pain for you.' So the player pulls down his shorts and she starts massaging his groin furiously.

'Thanks very much,' says the player when she's finished. 'But my ankle still hurts like hell.'

Man to Sunderland lass: 'Am I the first guy you ever made love to?'
Sunderland lass: 'Yeah, maybe. Your face definitely looks familiar.'

--- Newsflash

'David Beckham's voice is going to be used to make all stadium announcements at England's Euro 2004 matches.'
A spokesman said: 'We heard he comes over the PA really well.'

Q: Why did the Newcastle girl put ice in her pants?
A: To keep her crabs fresh.

International

Wayne Rooney goes into the England changing room and immediately notices that all his team mates are looking a bit agitated. 'What's wrong?' he asks.

'Well, we're having trouble getting motivated for this game,' says Beckham. 'We know it's important, but it's only Scotland. They're crap, and we can't really be bothered, to be honest.'

'Well, I reckon I can beat that shower on my own, so why don't you lads have the afternoon off and go to the pub?' says Rooney.

So the big striker runs out to take on the might of Scotland all by himself while his team mates pile off for a few pints. After a while, they ask the landlord to stick Teletext on to find out the score, and a great cheer goes up when the screen reads: England 1 (Rooney 10 minutes), Scotland 0.

An hour or so later, Beckham asks the landlord to put Teletext back on to see the final score. It reads: England 1 (Rooney 10 minutes), Scotland 1 (Angus McShite 89 minutes). The players are over the moon – the Boy Wonder has single-handedly secured a draw against Scotland's best eleven players!

They hurry back to the stadium to congratulate Rooney, but are surprised to find him in the dressing room crying into his shirt.

'I'm so sorry, lads, I've really let you down,' he sobs.

'Don't be stupid. You got a draw against Scotland all by yourself – and they only equalized in the eighty-ninth minute,' says Beckham.

'No, no, I really have let you down,' Rooney protests. 'I got sent off in the twelfth minute.'

Q: What do Scotland goalkeepers and Michael Jackson have in common?
A: Both wear gloves for no apparent reason.

A young Welsh apprentice is practising his free kicks at Aston Villa's training ground. First-team manager David O'Leary sees the boy curl a few into the corner of the net and wanders over to have a chat with the youngster.

'How old are you, son?' asks O'Leary.

'Thirteen,' the little boyo replies.

'Well, I am very impressed with your shooting ability,' continues the honey-voiced Irishman. 'If you can maintain this kind of form, when you get older you may be good enough to play for the Villa first team.'

'F**k off!' snaps the young lad. 'It's bad enough being Welsh.'

Q: What do you call a Wales fan with lots of lovers?
A: A shepherd.

Q. What do you call an Englishman in the final of the World Cup?
A. The referee.

Q: What is the main function of the Scotland coach?
A: To transport the team from the hotel to the ground and back.

Wales manager John Toshack calls his England counterpart Sven Goran Eriksson to ask him how to improve his training methods.

'Dustbins, my friend, for sure,' says Sven. 'Place them all around the pitch and get your players to pass the ball between them, dribble around them, lob and head the ball over them and so on. You'll find it'll improve the players' all-round game. For sure.'

The following day the phone rings and Sven picks it up. 'Hi, it's Tosh here, Sven. The dustbins are winning 3–0. What do I do now?'

Q: What's the difference between Germany goalkeeper Oliver Kahn and a taxi driver?
A: A taxi driver only lets in four at a time.

England captain David Beckham has grown fed up with everyone saying he's really thick, so he decides to go back to school for a brief period to brush up his education.

After a couple of weeks, Posh goes to pick him up one afternoon and asks the teacher: 'How's David been getting on?'

'Brilliantly,' says the teacher. 'He's achieved straight As.'

'That's tremendous,' replies Posh, patting David on the head.

'Yes, next week we are going to start work on his Bs.'

Q: What's the quickest way out of Wembley?
A: The Southgate.

(Joke by German caller (!!) to radio station after Gareth missed penalty in shootout of Euro 96 semi-final.)

David Beckham is driving down the motorway outside Madrid when his mobile phone rings. It's his wife Posh, who says: 'Be careful, David. I've just heard a report on the radio that some thicko's driving the wrong way down the motorway.'

'Well, that's just plain wrong, girl,' David squeaks. 'There's bloody thousands of them.'

Q: Why is the pitch at Hampden Park so green and lush?

A: Because they keep putting lots of shit on it.

Q: What do you call a Wales fan with five sheep?
A: A pimp.

David Beckham and the England boys head out to a bar for a post-match drink and they take a hippo along as company for Wayne Rooney. The hippo proceeds to drink eighteen pints and then falls flat on its face. As the players get up to go, the barman protests: 'Hey, you can't leave that lyin' on the floor!'

'It's not a lion, stupid, it's a hippo,' replies Beckham.

Two Wales fans called Dai and Gareth, both farmers, are flying with their herd of sheep to a new farm when the engine fails and the plane starts spiralling towards the ground.

'Quick! Grab a parachute and jump!' shouts Dai.

'What about the sheep?' screams Gareth.

'F**k the sheep!' bellows Dai.

'Do you think we have time?' replies Gareth.

Q: What's the difference between Scotland and a tea bag?
A: The tea bag stays in the cup longer.

A French fan walks into a bar with a toad on his head, and the barman says: 'What the bleeding hell is that?'

The toad replies: 'I have no idea. It started as a wart on my bum and just got bigger and bigger.'

Ronaldo, Luis Figo and David Beckham have gone to heaven and are standing before God.

'You are here today to face your Creator and reflect on your life. I shall ask each of you one question,' God booms. 'Ronaldo, one of the world's greatest football players, why do you think that you have won a place in heaven?'

'I believe football to be an inspiration for humanity, particularly for the poor and downtrodden. Football brings simple, unfettered joy to millions, from the garbage-tip slums of Rio to the sophisticated streets of Madrid and Milan. I have spent my entire life trying to bring this joy, this celebration of life, to all people everywhere.'

'Very eloquent, Ronaldo,' says God, turning his attention to Figo. 'And you, Luis, a hero to so many in spite of your oily hair, what do you think has brought you here today?'

Figo puffs out his chest and says: 'I believe courage, honour, respect and humility are the building blocks of humanity and I've spent my whole life trying to live up to those ideals.'

God is impressed by the Portuguese maestro and, after wiping away a tear, He turns to the England captain. 'Now, David, I presume you just want your ball back.'

(See Beckham's string of missed penalties for England.)

Q: What's the difference between O. J. Simpson and England?
A: O. J. Simpson had a more credible defence.

Rumours that David Beckham has been successfully seducing a young woman in a Spanish nightclub have been completely refuted by the English FA. A spokesman said in a statement: 'It is self-evidently absurd to suggest that David, or any other England international for that matter, is capable of making a successful pass at anyone.'

Did you hear about the politician who was found dead in a Welsh football jersey?

The police had to dress him up in women's underwear and pop a dead sheep in his bed in order to save his family from the embarrassment.

Q: How many Scots fans does it take to change a lightbulb?
A: One million. One to change it, and 999,999 to blame all the world's ills on the bloody English.

An English fan, an Irish fan and a Scots fan are in a pub, talking about their families.

'My son was born on St George's Day,' says the English fan. 'So we obviously decided to call him George.'

'That's a real coincidence,' says the Scot. 'My son was born on St Andrew's Day, so we decided to call him Andrew.'

'That's incredible. What a coincidence,' says the Irish fan. 'Exactly the same thing happened with my son Pancake.'

The Scotland team are in the dressing room at Wembley a few minutes before their crucial qualifier against England kicks off. The manager Jock McShite is pacing the floor and stabbing the air with his finger. 'Remember, lads,' says the coach. 'If you can't kick the ball, kick your opponent's shins, and if you can't kick his shins, trip him up and kick the bugger in the head. Now, pick up that ball and get out there.'

'Sod the ball,' shouts the captain Davie McKipper. 'Let's just get on with the game.'

Q: How many Irish fans does it take to change a lightbulb?

A: Thirty. One to change the bulb and twenty-nine to sing about the experience and cry into their pints.

Q: How many surreal Welshmen does it take to change a lightbulb?
A: Sheep.

Q: What's the difference between Wayne Rooney and a mini?
A: A mini can only carry three passengers.

An English fan, an Irish fan and a Scots fan are sitting in a bar laughing about how stupid their wives are.

The Englishman says: 'My wife is so dumb last week she went to the supermarket and bought 300 pounds' worth of meat because it was on special offer, and we don't even have a fridge to keep it in.'

The Scotsman says: 'Well, if you think that's bad, just yesterday mine went out and spent 20,000 pounds on a new car and the silly twit doesn't even know how to drive!'

The Irishman chuckles and says: 'I think I can top that. My wife has gone on holiday to Greece. I saw her packing a mega-pack of 100 condoms into her suitcase, and she doesn't even have a penis!'

Q: Why do French fans eat garlic?
A: To improve their breath.

Q: What do you call a Welsh fan with a sheep under one arm and a goat under the other?
A: A bisexual.

A German fan walks into a bar carrying a duck under his arm, and the bartender exclaims: 'Oi! You can't bring that pig in here.'

'Excuse me, but it's a duck, not a pig,' the German protests.

'I wasn't talking to you, I was talking to the duck.'

Q: Why did the French celebrate their World Cup triumph so wildly?
A: It was the first time they'd won anything without the help of the United States and Britain.

A French fan, an English fan and Claudia Schiffer are sitting together in a carriage in a train travelling through France. When the train enters a long tunnel the carriage is plunged into darkness. After a few moments there is a kissing noise, followed quickly by the sound of a stinging slap. When the train comes out of the tunnel, Claudia Schiffer and the Englishman are sitting as if nothing had happened and the Frenchman is rubbing his face.

The Frenchman is thinking: 'The English chap must have kissed Claudia Schiffer and she missed him and slapped me instead.'

Claudia Schiffer is thinking: 'The Frenchman must have tried to kiss me and actually kissed the Englishman and got slapped for it.'

The Englishman is thinking: 'This is great. The next time the train goes through a tunnel I'll make another kissing noise and slap that French bastard again.'

Did you hear the one about the Scotland fan who bought a round of drinks?

No.

Q. What's the difference between a Scotland fan and a coconut?
A. You can get a drink out of a coconut.

--- SKY Newsflash

A Glasgow taxi crashed into a lamp-post on the way to
Hampden Park for a Group D 'six pointer' against the
Faroe Islands. Twenty-two Scotland fans were taken to
hospital for treatment.

An Irish fan is late for the match and when he arrives midway through the
second half he turns to the man next to him and asks: 'What's the score?'
  'Nil–nil,' comes the reply.
  'And what about at half-time?'

England manager Sven Goran Eriksson spots a turd on the England
training pitch and says to the squad:
  'Who's sh*t on the pitch?'
  Emile Heskey replies: 'I am, boss, but I'm not bad in the air.'

A boat carrying fans to the World Cup finals is wrecked in a storm, and those lucky enough to survive are washed up on a desert island. Among them are:

Two Italian fans and an Italian woman,
Two French fans and a French woman,
Two Japan fans and a Japanese woman,
Two German fans and a German woman,
Two Greek fans and a Greek woman,
Two England fans and an English woman.

One month later, the situation is as follows:
One Italian man has killed the other in a row over the woman.
The two French fans and the French woman are living happily together, having loads of sex.
The two Germans have a strict weekly schedule of when to alternate with the German woman.
The two Japanese have faxed Tokyo and are waiting for further instructions.
The two Greeks are sleeping with each other, and the Greek woman is cleaning and cooking for them.
The two Englishmen are waiting for someone to introduce them to the English woman.

England manager Sven Goran Eriksson tells Wayne Rooney that he is going to play him in the upcoming England friendly but will probably pull him off at half time.

'That's very kind of you, Sven,' says Wayne. 'At United, all we get is a cup of tea and an orange!'

(Apologies to Sir Alf Ramsey and Rodney Marsh.)

Five Facts to Make a Dutch Fan Proud

1. You can make jokes about the Belgians and still drink their beer.
2. You're exactly like the Germans except nobody hates you.
3. You think you are a world power, but everyone else thinks Brussels is your capital.
4. You can put your finger in a dyke and save your country.
5. If the economy is bad, you can blame the Germans. If the weather is bad, you can blame the Germans. If you lose your glasses, blame the Germans.

Five Facts to Make a French Fan Proud

1. When speaking fast you sound gay.
2. If there's a war, you can surrender nice and early.
3. You don't have to read the subtitles on those exotic midnight films on Channel 5.
4. You can test your own nuclear weapons in other people's countries.
5. You can be ugly and still become a famous film star.

Five Facts to Make a Norwegian Fan Proud

1. You get to kill baby seals and whales for a laugh.
2. You can go skiing in your pants.
3. You get to hate the Swedes and beat the Brazilians in football.
4. You have to be a woman to get anywhere.
5. You can actually get bored with blondes.

Five Facts to Make an English Fan Proud

1. It beats being Scottish.
2. Marmite.
3. You get to accept defeat graciously in major sporting events.
4. Union Jack underpants.
5. It beats being Welsh.

Five Facts to Make a Scotland Fan Proud

1. You're not English.
2. You're not English.
3. You're not English.
4. You're not English.
5. You're not English.

Five Facts to Make an Italian Fan Proud

1. Glorious military history up to AD100.
2. You can wear sunglasses inside and no one laughs at you.
3. Centuries of political stability and a slick economy.
4. You live near the Pope.
5. You can while away the time on a long train journey braiding your girlfriend's armpit hair.

Five Facts to Make a German Fan Proud

1.
2.
3.
4.
5.

Five Facts to Make an Irish Fan Proud

1. Guinness.
2. You can get into a fight simply by marching down someone's road in a bowler hat.
3. You get to kill people you don't agree with.
4. Boiled bacon.
5. Guinness.

Football Agents

A football agent buys a country cottage as a weekend retreat for his family. On his first visit there they go for a walk after Sunday lunch. The agent steps in a cowpat and starts screaming: 'F**k! Someone help me! I'm melting.'

A football agent steps out of his X series BMW car, and the door is immediately ripped off by a passing vehicle. When the police arrive on the scene, the agent bleats: 'Look, officer, look what that bastard has done to my new car.'

'Blimey, you football agents are so greedy and materialistic you haven't even noticed that he's torn your arm off, too.'

'Shit, my Rolex Oyster!'

A man arrives at work with leaves, branches and blood all over the bonnet of his car.

'Wow, whatever happened to you?' asks a colleague.

'I hit a football agent on the way to work,' replies the man, stepping out of his car.

'Well, that explains the blood, but what about the branches and the leaves?' asks the colleague.

'He lost me in the park for a while.'

Q: How can you tell when a football agent is lying?
A: His lips are moving.

```
--- SKY Newsflash
- - - - - - - - - - - - - - - - -
```
Terrorists have kidnapped fifty football agents on the way to their annual convention. They are threatening to release them one by one until their demands are met.

Thieves burst into a football agents' office to seize as much cash as possible, but the agents fight back so furiously that the thieves have to beat an early retreat. In the getaway car, one thief says to the others: 'Well, the good news is that we have got a hundred quid here. The bad news is that we went in there with two hundred.'

Two alligators are walking along the riverbank and one keeps licking the other one's bum. 'Hey, will you stop doing that? It's really annoying,' says the one in front.

'Sorry, it's just that I ate a football agent for lunch and I'm trying to get the taste out of my mouth.'

Q: How do you stop a football agent from drowning?
A: Take your foot off his head.

Q: Why do they bury football agents in ten-foot holes?
A: Because deep down they're really nice people.

A primary-school teacher asks the children in her class what their parents do for a living.

'My daddy's a heart surgeon,' says Tommy.

'Ah, that's lovely,' says the teacher.

'My daddy's a fireman,' says Wendy.

'Ah, that's lovely. What a good man,' says the teacher.

'My mummy works with mentally disabled people,' says Harry.

'Ah, that's tremendous. What a saint,' says the teacher.

'My dad's a pimp and a crack dealer,' says Jimmy.

The teacher is appalled, and at the end of the school day she rings Jimmy's mummy to find out whether or not it is true.

Jimmy's mother sighs and says: 'It's not true. Actually Jimmy's dad is a football agent, but how do you explain that to a seven-year-old?'

Q. Why don't sharks ever attack football agents?
A. Professional courtesy.

Q. Why don't hyenas eat football agents?
A. Even hyenas have their dignity.

The Devil visits a football agent's office and makes him an offer. 'I can arrange some things for you,' the Devil tells him. 'I'll increase your income tenfold. Your partners will love you, your clients will respect you, you'll have four months of holiday a year and live to be a hundred years old. All I require in return are the souls of your mother, your wife, your children and your grandchildren to rot in Hell for all Eternity.'

  'What's the catch? asks the football agent.

Q: What's the difference between a football agent and a rhinoceros?
A: The agent charges more.

Q: Why did God make snakes just before football agents?
A: To practise.

Q: Why are there so many football agents in the UK?
A: Because St Patrick chased all the snakes out of Ireland.

Q: What do you call a criminal football agent?
A: Redundant.

A genocidal maniac dies and is welcomed to the fiery depths of Hell by the Devil. As he passes through the steaming pits and screaming sinners, he sees a man he recognizes as a football agent snuggling up to a beautiful woman.

'Why, that's so unfair!' he cries. 'I have to burn for all Eternity, and that fat, greedy football agent gets to spend it with a beautiful woman.'

'Shut up!' snaps the Devil, jabbing him with his fork. 'Who are you to question that woman's punishment?'

A blind bunny and a blind snake are born at the same time, and grow up together, becoming the best of friends. Neither one knows what kind of creature the other one is, and one day they decide to touch each other and describe the sensations. The snake goes first, saying: 'You're all furry, you have two ears and a fluffy little tail.'

The bunny is overjoyed and starts shouting: 'I'm a bunny, I'm a bunny!'

Then the bunny feels the snake, saying: 'You've got slimy skin, beady eyes and a forked tongue.'

The snake groans. 'Oh shit, I must be a football agent.'

An attractive woman with beautiful lips finds herself alone in a lift with a football agent. 'I could push this red button, get down on my knees and give you the best blow job of your life,' she purrs.

The agent thinks for a minute and says, 'I'm sure you could – but what's in it for me?'

Q: What's wrong with football agent jokes?
A: Football agents don't think they're funny, and nobody else thinks they're jokes.

Q: What do you throw a drowning football agent?
A: His colleagues.

Q: What do you say to a football agent when you see he's about to get hit by a lorry?
A:

Q: What's the difference between football agents and vampires?
A: Vampires only suck blood at night.

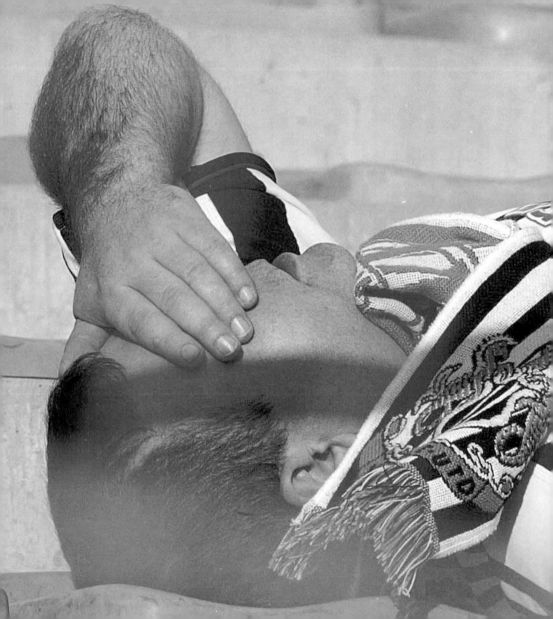

Q: Where can you find a good football agent?
A: In the cemetery.

A moral dilemma:

You are driving home from work and you see two football agents involved in a dreadful car accident. Both cars are ablaze, and both men are screaming for you to rescue them. But you only have time to rescue one before the cars blow up. What do you do? Go home and watch *Coronation Street*, or go to the pub for a pint?

Backwater Teams

BBC Newsflash

- - - - - - - - - - - - -

Thieves have broken into the home of a Norwich fan and stolen two books.

The fan told police: 'The thing that upsets me most is that I hadn't finished colouring them in yet.'

Q: What do you get if you cross an Ipswich fan with a pig?
A: Thick bacon.

Q: How can you tell a level-headed Torquay supporter?
A: He dribbles from both sides of his mouth.

Q: Santa Claus, the Easter bunny, an intelligent Ipswich supporter and an old drunk are walking down the street together when they spot a fifty-pound note on the ground. Who gets it?
A: The old drunk – the other three are mythical creatures.

Q: How do you confuse a Plymouth fan?
A: Show him a map of Plymouth.

Q: How do you make a Norwich fan laugh on a Saturday?
A: Tell him a joke on Monday.

Q: What do you get when you cross a Plymouth fan with a pig?
A: I don't know – there are some things a pig just won't do.

Q: How do you define 144 Wrexham fans?
A: Gross stupidity.

Two Norwich fans are on a plane heading to the Med for their holiday. One turns to the other and says: 'Hey, Giles, if this plane turns upside-down will we fall out?

'No way, Jethro,' says the other. 'Of course we'll still be pals.'

Q: What's the difference between a Carlisle fan and a coconut?
A: One's thick and hairy, and the other's a tropical fruit.

Q: How can you tell ET is a Grimsby fan?
A: Because he looks like one.

Q: How did the Exeter fan find his sister in the woods?
A: Just great.

Q: What did the Swindon lass say when the doctor told her she was pregnant?
A: Are you sure it's mine?

A Wigan fan reaches a riverbank when he spots another Wigan fan on the opposite bank. 'Hey,' he shouts, 'how can I get to the other side?' The other Wigan fan looks perplexed and shouts back: 'You *are* on the other side, you stupid twat.'

Q: How did the Yeovil fan die drinking milk?
A: The cow sat on him.

A Chester fan says to his mate: 'It's really weird but I keep seeing all these spots in front of my eyes.'
   'Have you seen a doctor yet?' the mate asks.
   'No, so far it's just been the spots.'

A hungry Norwich fan leaves Carrow Road and heads into a pizza takeaway at the end of the match.

'Do you want that cut into four or eight slices?' asks the pizza man.

'Eight? I'm not that hungry, mate. Just the four, please.'

A Burnley fan is walking down the road outside Turf Moor dragging a long piece of string.

Intrigued, an onlooker asks him: 'Why are you pulling that bit of string?'

'Because it's a damned sight easier than pushing it, let me tell you.'

A Norwich fan is walking to the match at Carrow Road when he spots a banana skin fifty yards down the road from him. 'Oh f**k! Here we go again,' he sighs.

Two Ipswich fans are on the way out of Portman Road when one of them spots a mirror on the ground. He picks it up and looks into it, saying: 'Hey, I think I know that bloke. His face really rings a bell.'

His mate grabs it off him and has a look himself before replying: 'Of course you do, you thick bastard – it's me!'

Q: What do you call a Carlisle fan with two brain cells?
A: Pregnant.

A Shrewsbury fan comes across a soft-drinks machine on his way out of Gay Meadow International Arena. He puts in some money, and a can falls down into the tray at the bottom. He then puts in some more coins, then some more, then some more … until a man in the queue behind him says: 'For God's sake, isn't that enough yet?'

'Shut up,' replies the Shrewsbury fan. 'Can't you see I'm winning?'

Magistrate: What is your date of birth?
Northampton fan: August 7th.
Magistrate: What year?
Northampton fan: Every year.

An anxious woman goes to her doctor. 'Doctor, I'm a little worried – can you get pregnant from anal intercourse?'

'Of course you can,' replies the good doctor. 'Where do you think Walsall fans come from?'

Q: What do you get when you put twenty-eight Norwich fans in one room?
A: A full set of teeth.

Q: Who's the poorest person in Bristol?
A: The tooth fairy.

A newspaper reporter is interviewing some Yeovil fans before a big FA Cup match, and says to one of them: 'There are some people who live in the big cities who think that you country folk like to have sex with farm animals like cows, pigs and chickens. What do you say to that kind of innuendo and allegation?'

'Chickens? What kind of a sick pervert has sex with chickens?' replies the man.

Q: What do you call a Grimsby fan with an IQ of ten?
A: A Grimsby fan.

Q: What's the most popular chat-up line in Bristol?
A: 'Nice tooth, love.'

Q: How many Burnley fans does it take to change a lightbulb?
A: Change it to what?

Q: How do you know if a Norwich fan has been using your computer?
A: There's cheese in front of the mouse.

You know you are an Ipswich fan if ...

(a) You can't marry your childhood sweetheart because there is a law against it.

(b) Your family tree goes in a straight line.

(c) Your car is immobile but your house isn't it.

(d) Your wife has hives on her beer belly and you find that horny.

(e) You use axle grease as a sexual lubricant.

(f) You come back from the dump with more than you take.

(g) You've been involved in a custody battle over a sheep.

(h) Your teacher says: 'Always remember it's I before E except in Budweiser.'

You know you're a Norwich fan if ...

(a) You can gob without opening your mouth.

(b) You hit on girls in the VD clinic.

(c) The biggest city you've been to after Norwich is Kings Lynn.

(d) You have been excused jury service because it clashed with a GCSE exam.

(e) Your wife climbs trees for fun.

(f) You come over all dreamy and romantic when you are herding your cows.

(g) You give your family items of livestock for Christmas.

Q: Why should you not allow Reading fans a coffee break at work?
A: Because it takes too long to retrain them.

A Darlington fan is to meet his new girlfriend outside the cinema at six o'clock. By nine she has still not arrived, so he goes home fuming. Later he phones her up and says: 'Where the hell were you? I waited for two hours in the cold before leaving.'

The girl replies: 'I'm not going out with you now – we're finished.'

'Why's that?' he asks.

'One of my friends told me you're a paedophile,' she replies.

'Paedophile?' cries the incredulous Darlington fan. 'That's a big word for a seven-year-old.'

Q. How does a Tranmere fan get into an honest business?
A. Through the skylight.

Q: What job do you give a Bristol Rovers fan at an M&M factory?
A: Proofreader.

Q: Why did the Bristol Rovers fan get sacked from the M&M factory?
A: Because he kept throwing away the Ws.

Q: What's half a mile long and has an IQ of forty?
A: The queue for the turnstiles at Derby.

Q: How did the Lincoln City fan kill himself raking leaves?
A: He fell out of the tree.

Two Chesterfield fans are walking down the road, and the first says: 'Hey, look at that dog over there with one eye!'
  So the other Spireite covers one of her eyes and says: 'Where?'

A Burnley fan is walking down the street with a pig under his arm when a passer-by stops and asks: 'Where did you get that from?'
  The pig replies: 'I won it in a raffle!'

Q: Why don't Norwich fans eat pickled onions?
A: Because they can't get their heads in the jar.

Q: Why don't Ipswich fans like Smarties?
A: Because they're so hard to peel.

Q: How did the Grimsby fan get twenty-eight holes in his face?
A: He was trying to eat with a fork.

Q: How do Norwich fans spell farm?
A: E-I-E-I-O.

Q: How do you recognize a Norwich fan at the airport?
A: He's the one throwing bread at the airplanes.

Q: How many Norwich City fans does it take to play hide-and-seek?
A: One.

Q: How do we know that the toothbrush was invented in Bristol?
A: Because if it was invented anywhere else it would be known as a 'teethbrush'.

Q: What's the difference between a Wrexham fan and a baboon?
A: One's hairy, stupid and smells, and the other is a baboon.